THIEVING ANIMALS

Consultant: Steve Pollock
Graphic design: Sandra Brys

© Casterman 1993
First published in the UK in 1994 by
Belitha Press Ltd
31 Newington Green, London N16 9PU
© First published in French by
Casterman 1993

ISBN 1 855 61 311 5

THIEVING ANIMALS

Robert Henno
Illustrated by Jean-Marie Winants
Consultant: Steve Pollock

CONTENTS

Belitha Press

All animals need food to survive. It is essential for young animals to eat so that they may grow. Food also provides just as much energy for fully-grown animals as it does for their young, so that they can move about and carry out their daily routines.

Where to find food

Green plants can make their own food from water and sunlight. Animals, on the other hand, must find food that is ready to be eaten. In general, the choice is limited to eating plants or other animals. Animals can be classified into five large groups:

- herbivores: they eat only plant life.
- insectivores: they only eat insects.
- carnivores: they capture living prey, and eat it immediately.
- scavengers: they eat other dead animals.
- omnivores: they eat both plants and animals.

INTRODUCTION

HOW ANIMALS FIND FOOD

Thieves

Animals use a lot of energy finding enough food to survive. They use even more energy when they have to provide for their young. They will take food wherever they find it, especially from convenient places, such as farms, where there are lots of food sources in one place. Farmers become angry with the animals that do this and call them thieves.

Food sources

Animals gather together in groups such as flocks or herds for protection. Birds may nest together in a colony. This group is a natural source of food for an animal that eats birds.

No colony can ever be totally safe from predators, particularly those that have become expert at raiding nests. But having access to such a colony does not always mean an easy life for the predator. In nature the number of predators is always controlled by the number of prey. If there is less prey, predators have fewer young, so their numbers are reduced. There are always fewer predators than prey.

Food stores

The most valuable stores of food for animals are sometimes created by people. For a rat or a mouse, a barn filled with grain or a cupboard filled with food is nothing less than a treasure trove! Faced with so much food, the only problem is choosing where to begin their meal. To a fox, a hen is easy prey. Hen runs are often very badly made, so it is much easier for a fox to hunt there than to run after a rabbit. Fish-breeding ponds overflow with fish. So it is easier for a heron to fish there than wait for hours at the edge of a river. These animals cannot be blamed for taking food which is easily available.

Is thieving harmful?

Some animals do steal from human food stores. But this does not always cause much harm. Those that do steal from us – such as voles, field mice and rats, are themselves often eaten by foxes and stoats. But some species cause great hardship to humans – such as African locusts. Locusts can cause famine in some regions of the world. Rats and mice, apart from the damage they cause, can also carry terrible diseases. But humans often help them, without realising it, to live in huge numbers. Some species find public rubbish dumps great sources of food. And their natural predators are often hunted so they no longer play their part in keeping down the animals' population.

THE MAGPIE

Near our house there are a couple of magpies that never stop squawking. At the beginning of spring, their life was not easy. They had to face a good many problems to protect their nest and young.

First they built a nest in one of the great poplars that border the fields. There are lots of worms, slugs, beetles and other insects, the magpies' favourite food, in that area. But a group of crows had discovered them first and thought of them as their territory. They did not stop bombarding the magpies, even attacking their nest, though it was very high in the tree. Finally, the magpies had to abandon their nest and went to a small public park. They decided to live in an old chestnut tree. But they had not counted on the jays! These squawking birds rush out of the woods on numerous raids. They started to attack the magpies immediately. So the magpies had to move again.

The magpies have built their third nest at the top of a fir tree. All around are small gardens and well-mown lawns. Finally left in peace, they lay and **incubate** their eggs.

Only a few days after hatching, the chicks cry out for food, with their large beaks open. How can their parents satisfy them? The magpie parents walk all around the lawn. They have examined the ground well and carefully inspected the flower beds, but the food that they take to the nest is not enough for their offspring.

They have no choice but to attack weaker birds. They have picked out the small song birds which shelter in the clipped hedges and trimmed shrubs. One by one, the nests of blackbirds, thrushes, chaffinches and warblers are raided. Everything goes, the eggs as well as the young birds.

But the magpies are not completely safe! A few people in the neighbourhood, who don't understand how difficult it is for these birds to survive, decide to stop this 'murder'. They try to shoot the magpies.

LOCATION	DESCRIPTION	ENVIRONMENT	HABITS AND BEHAVIOUR

LOCATION

● The magpie is found throughout Europe, with the exception of Iceland and some Mediterranean islands. Its close relative, the azure magpie, is found in the centre and south of Spain, as well as in Portugal.

DESCRIPTION

● The magpie's black and white **plumage** and long, wedge-shaped tail make it an easily identifiable bird. Its black feathers seem to reflect purples, blues and greens.

● It is between 40-46 cm long, half of which is the tail.

● The azure magpie is clearly different and smaller, being only 35 cm long. It has a white breast, its head is covered with a black hood, its tail and wings are blue and the rest of the bird is grey.

ENVIRONMENT

● The magpie lives in open landscapes with well-spaced trees, woods and farms. It is happy to live near villages and even the suburbs of towns and city parks.

● It is not found in dense forest or at **altitudes** of over 1,500 metres.

HABITS AND BEHAVIOUR

● Magpies stick to the same territory. They move about a lot in this area depending on the seasons, especially between January and March. During this time they move about in small groups and chatter non-stop. They chase each other in crazy and noisy games. Without stopping, they hop from tree to tree and jump from branch to branch.

● Their cry is a 'chak-chak-chak-chak', which is not even vaguely tuneful. In the nesting season they produce more varied sounds and whistles.

DIET

● The magpie can eat almost anything. It mainly eats **invertebrates** (insects, **larvae**, worms, slugs, snails and spiders). Every now and then it will add a small lizard or rodent to its diet. It is known to attack sick or injured domestic animals and will also feed from carcasses. They can eat plants, grain and fruit, as well as acorns, nuts, peas and sometimes potatoes.

● Magpies and crows have a very similar diet. Constant stealing makes them competitors for territory. Jays are also competitors with magpies. Jays are less possessive of their territory than magpies and may leave the forest edge in groups to visit the food sources of their neighbours.

REPRODUCTION

● The magpie's nest is normally built at the top of a tall tree or in a thorny bush. The nest is large and made of small dry branches. It has an outer framework of sticks and large twigs and has a heavy mud cap inside lined with fine roots, hair and grass stems. Sometimes the whole thing is covered with a dome of thorny twigs, in which there are a few holes for entrances.

● The magpie lays its eggs in April. There are about 5-7 eggs in the clutch. They are brownish green or blue, spotted with olive brown. Their incubation lasts 17-18 days.

● The chicks stay in the nest for 22-27 days and then stay with their parents until the end of summer.

THE MAGPIE AND PEOPLE

● The magpie has gradually come to live closer to people. It is easily spotted because of its dark outline, striking plumage, its clumsiness both on the ground and in flight, and most particularly its constant chattering. It has become the symbol of chattering and gossiping. It is also seen as a thief. This accusation is exaggerated. However, the magpie does like to line its nest with shiny objects - this often means that it takes shiny things from gardens or even houses. Today, people hate the magpie because it steals other birds' eggs. They see the magpie as harmful to other birds and would like to see its numbers limited.

DANGERS AND MEASURES FOR CONSERVATION

● The magpie has increasingly established itself closer and closer to human homes in artificial environments. However, their prey is less numerous in gardens with well-kept lawns, trimmed hedges made up of one type of plant, and cultivated bushes and shrubs.

● Because magpies live in these areas they are becoming more predatory towards other birds and their eggs.

● A different approach to gardening would stop the pillaging. People with gardens need to think about the effect they have on an environment and its wildlife.

THE FOX

Peter daydreams in his room. He has to finish an essay and the page in front of him is still totally blank. Suddenly he hears a commotion coming from the hen house. Peter rushes over to the window just in time to see a fox running off with a hen in its mouth. What a splendid animal! It has a coat of smooth honey red and a long bushy tail that lightly waves behind it. The fox stops for an instant, making sure it has a tight grip on the hen, turns its small triangular head towards the house, then slides beneath the garden fence and disappears into the tall grass.

Peter and his mother examine the hen house. The chicken wire is old and full of holes. It really should be replaced very soon. But Peter's father, away on a trip, is not coming home for another week, and this is the second hen that the fox has stolen.

What should they do? They try to think of possible solutions. A trap, or poison? These are out of the question.

Peter has the idea of frightening the fox, or worrying it. 'How?' says his mother. 'We guard the hen house day and night!'

'What if I set up my radio in the hen house? I could turn on the station that plays continuous music. I bet that will work. It would only cost us the price of a few batteries.' Peter's mother smiles. But Peter sticks to his idea and soon the chickens are listening to continuous pop music.

A few days have passed. The fox has not reappeared and Peter is jubilant, proud of his stroke of inspiration. And the cockerel, who hardly crowed before, has been inspired by the musical competition and now crows all day long.

On his return, Peter's father has a good laugh at the solution conjured up by his son. Together they replaced the chicken wire. Peter, who had not forgotten his work, finished his essay. The title was 'Craftier than a Fox.'

LOCATION	DESCRIPTION	ENVIRONMENT	HABITS AND BEHAVIOUR	DIET

LOCATION	DESCRIPTION	ENVIRONMENT	HABITS AND BEHAVIOUR	DIET
• The fox is found all over Europe except in Iceland and Crete.	• The fox's head and body measure 58-77 cm long; its tail is 32-48 cm long and it stands 35-40 cm high. • The male weighs 7 kg, and sometimes up to 10-12 kg; the female weighs 5-6 kg. • The outline of the fox is well known. At times people think it is larger than it actually is. This is because in a cold winter the fox fluffs out its fur for extra warmth. Its coat is usually red, but individual foxes can be more yellow, or more brown, or sometimes almost black. The Arctic fox or the blue fox lives in Iceland and the mountains of Scandinavia. It is smaller than the red fox and its coat turns white in winter.	• The fox can live in all sorts of environments. It is usually found in forests and their surroundings, but also in plains and mountainous areas. It likes to live in undergrowth, among stones and ruins. Today it can be seen in the suburbs of towns and even in city parks.	• The fox is especially active from sunset to dawn. Sometimes it can be seen during the day, especially when it is feeding its young. • Generally it hunts alone. Its territory varies in size from 300 to 400 hectares on average. • Several individuals sometimes form a group, which is looked after by both a **dominant** male and female. The edges of the group's territory is clearly marked out, often by **excrement**. • The fox has a variety of cries: hoarse, plaintive barks, short yaps and sometimes repeated yelping. It growls when frightened or on the attack.	• The fox has a very varied diet. Its basic diet is small rodents, particularly voles. If the chance arises, the fox will attack a rabbit, a hare or a pheasant. It also likes small birds and their chicks, fish, lizards, insects, snails and earthworms. Plants are also important in its diet: grapes, cherries, blackberries, prunes, tender ears of corn or wheat, certain grasses and wild berries. Carcasses are another source of food: the fox often picks up animals killed on the road. On the outskirts of towns and cities the fox will raid rubbish bins as well.

REPRODUCTION

- The female fox is **on heat** from January to February.
- The **gestation** period lasts about two months.
- Foxes rarely dig out a den for themselves. They move into an unoccupied or abandoned one (a rabbit's or a badger's). The young are born blind and weigh around 100 g. They are nursed for about 20 days.
- They are **weaned** gradually. They get some food from their mother which she has already chewed and swallowed. At 6-7 weeks, they are fully weaned. Shortly afterwards they follow their mother and learn to hunt.
- They become totally independent around September to October.

THE FOX AND PEOPLE

- The fox has an important place in people's imaginations. Stories and tales about their hunting are often full of exaggerated scenes. These tales often give the fox human behaviour and characteristics. Unfortunately these are often unpleasant characteristics, such as cunning, falseness, craftiness, and so on.
- People do not often see the fox's need to hunt birds or small game in an unbiased way. They see the fox as a cruel murderer because it kills efficiently.

What people forget is that the fox has to eat. And if it did not hunt there would be far too many rodents, such as mice and voles. The occasional killing of hens which are easy game to the fox should not allow us to forget that a fox may also kill up to 6,000 mice and small rodents a year.

DANGERS AND MEASURES FOR CONSERVATION

- In most parts of Europe, the fox no longer has natural enemies, such as wolves, lynxes, eagle owls and golden eagles. Although it is not threatened by extinction it should not be mercilessly hunted by people.
- The fox is, however, a principal **carrier** of rabies. Because it infects both people and other animals with this disease, there are campaigns in various areas to wipe it out. It has been hunted, trapped, poisoned and gassed from its den. Today most of these practices have now disappeared and a vaccine against rabies has been introduced.

Concealed in bait, the vaccine is distributed in areas frequented by the fox. The first results of this form of vaccination are encouraging.

THE HERON

John and Maggie gobble down their breakfast. Yesterday their grandmother had given them some goldfish and they were impatient to go and admire them. Hastily swallowing their last mouthful, they run to the far end of the garden and sit on the edge of the pond. They throw some small pieces of bread into the water and soon the fish come to the surface, rising to the bait. How many are there? 1, 2, 3, 4 . . . and 5! Repeated counting always gives them the same result. Worried, they count again one more time: half the fish have definitely disappeared. But there are no dead fish floating on the surface. They had noticed two fish missing yesterday evening. Mush, the neighbours' cat, could be behind the theft. But how, when the water is over 50 cm deep?

Determined to find out who the thief is, they decide to hide in the small shed at the far end of the garden. Over an hour goes by and nothing happens. The waiting starts to be boring. All of a sudden, they hear something above them. 'There is something on the roof,' whispers Maggie. With his finger over his lips, her brother silently orders her to be quiet. Less than two minutes later, a shadow appears on the lawn and a large bird comes to rest near the pond. It is a heron. It seems to be on the alert and keeps turning to the left and right. Reassured by the silence in the garden, the bird begins to preen its feathers. Its long neck curves in all directions. Suddenly it stops preening: its eye has been caught by a movement on the surface of the water. Automatically, it approaches the pond with slow and jerky steps. It moves into the water and freezes. Nothing happens. The bird could almost be stuffed, it is so still.

The minutes pass. The children hold their breath. Suddenly, the bird plunges its head beneath the water's surface. It pulls its head out of the water. At the end of its long beak one of the goldfish wriggles. The bird throws it into the air, catches it and swallows it head first. 'My fish,' shouts Maggie. Frightened, the heron takes flight.

LOCATION	DESCRIPTION	ENVIRONMENT	HABITS AND BEHAVIOUR

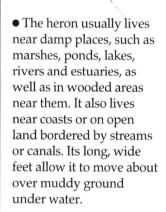

LOCATION

• The heron lives throughout most of Europe. It does not live in Iceland, and in Scandinavia it only lives in coastal regions. It lives in the northern parts of Europe during nesting periods and **migrates** south in winter to avoid the cold weather.

DESCRIPTION

• Grey is the main colour in the heron's plumage. Its neck is white, and the feathers at the tip of its wings are black. A black line also runs down its neck. Adult herons have a black band above their eye that extends to the crest that covers its head.
• It has a thin head and a long slender beak.
• It has long thin legs.
• Size:
- length: 90 cm
- wingspan: 1.50 m.
The common heron is the largest of the European herons.
• In flight its neck is folded into an S-shape.

ENVIRONMENT

• The heron usually lives near damp places, such as marshes, ponds, lakes, rivers and estuaries, as well as in wooded areas near them. It also lives near coasts or on open land bordered by streams or canals. Its long, wide feet allow it to move about over muddy ground under water.

HABITS AND BEHAVIOUR

• The common heron lives alone as well as in groups. It is especially active during the day. At times it may also hunt and fly around sunset.
• Its flight is low and heavy. It flaps its wings as if it were moving in slow motion. Unlike other waders, such as the stork, it glides in flight. Its curved wings distinguish it from other birds of prey which fly with their wings spread wide open.

• The heron does not hide and can easily be spotted in the places that it lives. Perched in a tree with its wings slightly spread open, it likes to sunbathe.
• When it is startled the heron takes flight letting out a 'crah' sound. The same cry is regularly called in flight. In nesting areas it utters a cackling, 'kakaka'.

DIET

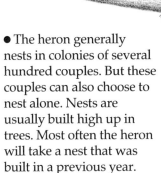

● The diet of the heron is very varied. It feeds on frogs, tadpoles, eels, small fish, voles and even small snakes. It mainly hunts from a hiding place and can remain still for very long periods of time, watching carefully for its prey. The prey is not caught by piercing, but is seized in the heron's beak. With a quick flick, the fish is thrown into the air, caught and immediately swallowed head first. Some prey that are too large or put up a good fight cannot easily be swallowed. The bird brings them to the bank where they are beaten to death and then eaten.

REPRODUCTION

● The heron generally nests in colonies of several hundred couples. But these couples can also choose to nest alone. Nests are usually built high up in trees. Most often the heron will take a nest that was built in a previous year.
● The female lays from 2 to 6 eggs of a bright green-blue colour. The egg laying season begins around the end of February and the beginning of March. Incubation lasts for 24-28 days and is done by both parents. They also raise their chicks together. After about 20 days the chicks perch on the edge of their nest and on neighbouring branches. They do not leave the nest until 50-55 days after hatching.

THE COMMON HERON AND PEOPLE

● The heron's taste for fish has annoyed fishermen and fish breeders. They were classified as harmful birds, and frequently killed. During the 1950s, there were so few herons that people were afraid the species would not survive. Then a study of their habits showed that herons had almost no effect on fish breeding populations. In Germany a dead heron was found with more than 20 voles. in its stomach

● Today, this bird is protected in a number of countries. Its numbers are building up again. Little by little the heron has lost its fear of people and some birds live in cities. Some herons find food in fish ponds. They also beg anglers for the small fish that they do not want.

DANGERS AND MEASURES FOR CONSERVATION

● The heron likes to frequent fish ponds. It finds a large number of prey easy to catch there. Some fish breeders continue to hunt it, with little regard for the laws that protect the birds. There are ways of protecting the fish, such as shooting blanks to frighten herons away with the noise, or by placing nets on pond banks.

Antoine, Anne, and François were extremely excited. They had just returned from the village where their mother had sent them on a few errands and were saying that they had seen 'several creatures', running around the roof of an old house. 'They were rather large,' said Antoine, 'like cats, but shorter and longer. We could not see them well because it was getting dark.'

'I was afraid,' said Anne. 'When they noticed us, they stopped abruptly. Then they began to run away on to the other slope of the roof.' The children's mother did not completely believe this story. They had a tendency to invent so much! 'Sit at the table, supper is ready. And stop your nonsense right now! You can tell your father, when he comes home!'

François, the youngest, said nothing. But just as his mother sat him at the table and tied a bib around his neck, he declared. 'I saw them as well, the beasts were going to eat too, they had put on their bibs!' Everyone laughed, except for François, who was annoyed.

THE STONE MARTEN

When their father returned, he did not seem surprised. He listened to the children's story and congratulated François for his remark. 'You must have seen a family of stone martens,' he concluded. 'They are very pretty. Their coats are brown and beige and they have a white spot on their neck and chest, like a napkin or bib. You mustn't be afraid of them. They are very skilful and mischievous animals. They are like acrobatic clowns; they love playing games and doing somersaults. If you like, we will try to see them again one night. But we must keep absolutely still and silent, because they are suspicious of people. People sometimes tell ghost stories about them. Often the high-pitched cries of the stone martens and their noisy games led people to believe that a house was haunted. The owners of the house, who sometimes only saw the stone martens by chance during the day, could not imagine that when night came, the same animals made such a noise! Now off to bed all of you – and don't upset the ghosts!'

LOCATION

• The stone marten is spread throughout continental Europe. It is not found in Ireland, Great Britain, Iceland and Scandinavia. To the south it does not live in Corsica, Sardinia, and Sicily, though it does live on other islands, such as the Balearics, Corfu, Cyprus, Rhodes and Crete.

DESCRIPTION

• Like most of the weasel family, the stone marten has a long, lithe body with short legs and a pointed nose. Its back is slightly curved.
• Its fur varies from a brown to a greyish-beige colour.
• The stone marten's head and body is 41-49 cm; its tail is 23-26 cm and it stands around 12 cm high.
• The male weighs 1.7 to 2.5 kg and the female is lighter at 1.1 to 1.5 kg.
• The stone marten can be confused with the pine marten, which has a slightly darker coat.

ENVIRONMENT

• The stone marten has a special affection for human habitats. It can be found in attics, barns, hay lofts, wood piles, ruins and old walls. Unlike the pine marten, which only lives in forests, the stone marten prefers to live on the edge of a wood near people.
• In southern Europe, it lives further away from houses, usually in rocky or stony places.

HABITS AND BEHAVIOUR

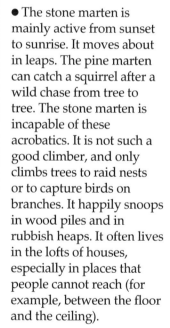

• The stone marten is mainly active from sunset to sunrise. It moves about in leaps. The pine marten can catch a squirrel after a wild chase from tree to tree. The stone marten is incapable of these acrobatics. It is not such a good climber, and only climbs trees to raid nests or to capture birds on branches. It happily snoops in wood piles and in rubbish heaps. It often lives in the lofts of houses, especially in places that people cannot reach (for example, between the floor and the ceiling).

• Stone martens are rather noisy, especially when it is warm and the young grow up. In houses, the noise caused by the games of the young often worry the inhabitants. The stone marten has a wide variety of cries; growling when it is uneasy, as well as making yapping, whistling, and piercing cries.

DIET

● The stone marten is classified as a **carnivore**. In reality it is omnivorous and adapts its diet to the season. Its basic diet is small rodents, such as mice, voles, and rats (sewer rats in the city). It sometimes takes birds out of their nests. It also eats insects and earthworms.

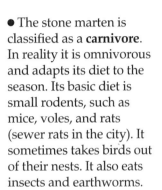

● During the summer and autumn, most of its food comes from plants (apples, pears, cherries, and so on). It loves eggs and may also raid hen houses, pigeon lofts and rabbit hutches, slaughtering the animals inside.

REPRODUCTION

● Although mating takes place in the summer, the young are not born until April or May. After the eggs are **fertilised** by the male, they are stored for several months inside the mother's body. The **embryos** do not begin to develop until they are **implanted** in the **uterus**. The true gestation period is only about 2 months.
● The females have between 1 to 5 young. They are born naked and blind. They are weaned after 6 to 7 weeks and are fed with prey brought in by their mother. At the age of 3 months, they can hunt for themselves.
● When females are on heat, they can be found easily by their cries and by the noise of their games.

STONE MARTENS AND PEOPLE

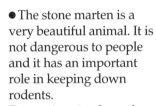

● The stone marten spends most of its time capturing rodents that live in and around houses. It is the main predator of the brown rat and even cats are afraid of being attacked by it.

● Although the stone marten is useful to people, it has a bad reputation. This is for two main reasons:
- it frightens people with its cries and the noise it makes during the night in attics and lofts;
- it kills domestic animals such as hens.

ROLE

● The stone marten is a very beautiful animal. It is not dangerous to people and it has an important role in keeping down rodents.
Domestic animals can be protected from a stone marten's raids by a wire fence with fairly small mesh. As it is good at climbing, it is best to cover the roof of any **aviary**. The cries and the noises made by its young should not be frightening. But when the animals live between the floor and the ceiling, these noises can be highly unpleasant. It is best to keep them out by sealing off entrances to the roof. But do not do this when the stone martens are there or during their breeding time.

THE HOUSE MOUSE

The mouse slowly and suspiciously circles the trap, sniffing at it. The piece of cheese that is fixed upon it as bait looks most appetising. Only a few days ago it saw one of its sisters get caught in a similar spring trap. Its neck was broken and it died from the blow. Although this mouse has been very successful at pinching bait in the past, it is careful. It draws back a little, jumps forward, hits the trap and leaps back immediately. Nothing happens.
It repeats the same moves from a different angle. This time the trap moves a few millimetres, but does not release the cheese. After a new and thorough inspection, the mouse makes a fresh attempt.
A snapping crack breaks the silence. The spring whisks past the tip of the mouse's nose as it leaps backwards. It comes so close that it catches a few of the mouse's whiskers. Immediately the mouse begins to nibble at the end of the cheese that remains fixed to the mousetrap.

As soon as it has finished eating, the mouse cleans itself vigorously and sets off again. Without stopping, it passes straight by the saucer filled with poisoned seeds. It has been a long time since it has even sniffed at this dangerous bait. A scampering noise behind it makes it stop. It turns its head and sees a young mouse heading towards the seeds. It has a starved air. The mouse retraces its steps and makes the young mouse understand that these seeds, despite their tempting appearance, must not be eaten.

A few minutes later its travels lead it to the door of the store cupboard, where food is kept. It creeps under the door. Bottles are arranged along one wall. But the mouse is not interested in these. It hungrily eyes the shelves, where there are boxes and packages that might be hiding a multitude of delicious morsels.

But how can it get up there? The step ladder that was against the wall yesterday has disappeared. Could it jump up to the first shelf? Impossible! It looks up and sees a cord running across the room, where bunches of onions have been hung up to dry. So it begins to climb the bottles placed against the wall. It climbs up from bottle to bottle. A last pull-up, a jump, and it reaches the cord. On this tightrope, it crosses the room. It loses its balance several times but manages to hang on, and finally reaches the food. It settles down to enjoy its hard won meal.

LOCATION	DESCRIPTION	ENVIRONMENT	HABITS AND BEHAVIOUR

LOCATION

- Originally the house mouse lived on the Asiatic plains, in north Africa and on the edge of the Mediterranean.
- Today the mouse lives throughout Europe.

DESCRIPTION

- The house mouse weighs 10-15 g.
- Its body without its tail measures about 7 to10 cm. The mouse's tail varies in length. Usually it is slightly longer than its body.
- Mice which live in houses are charcoal grey in colour. Those that live outside are usually fawn brown. Those that live outside should not be confused with field mice. The field mouse has much larger ears and eyes than the house mouse.

ENVIRONMENT

- The mouse has always lived with humans. During prehistoric times it was already sharing their shelters. But it is not an animal that has been domesticated by people, who have no use for it. Mouse families live in barns, attics, basements, and similar places. Some spend the winter inside, and go outside in the summer, living in gardens or in the open countryside.

HABITS AND BEHAVIOUR

- Mice live in family groups that vary in number. They are led by a dominant male who is generally stronger than the others. The members of the same group recognise each other by smell.

- Mice usually stay hidden during the day, although they can be active during the day too. They are most active at sunset or when humans go to bed. They are clever at avoiding being caught in traps.

DIET

- Originally mice ate only seeds and insects.
- Over time mice have become omnivorous. They now eat any food. They especially like things like paper, leather and soap!
- Mice which live in houses don't make stores of food, but go out in search of it every day. Those that live in the countryside build up stocks that last them during the winter months.

REPRODUCTION

- If mice live in good conditions (away from the cold and with plenty of food), they will reproduce all year round. Otherwise they reproduce between spring and autumn.
- Litters can be from 4 to 10 young (sometimes more). Their nest is made of anything the female can find, such as straw, hay, pieces of cloth, and so on.
- The young can feed themselves at 18 days old and can breed at 2 months old. A female could have 10 litters per year. But usually they average at about 5. The ability to reproduce so easily could cause overpopulation. So they limit themselves to only five litters a year.

MICE AND PEOPLE

- Mice can cause a lot of damage to the houses that they occupy: they can gnaw holes in walls, floors, and furniture. They use their teeth to tear the toughest materials. Rodents' teeth never stop growing, so they are used constantly. They steal a large quantity of food and waste a lot more by making it unfit for humans to eat.
- Like the rat, the mouse can also carry illnesses that are dangerous to people. So it has always been hunted. Its cleverness in escaping traps and other attempts to destroy it have made it a difficult animal to wipe out. Its natural predators (the cat, stone marten, and barn owl) all help to keep its numbers down.

THE WHITE MOUSE

- The white mouse is the albino form of the house mouse. The Egyptians were breeding it several thousands of years ago. Today it is the animal most often used to test medicines in laboratories. Each year, several million white mice are used in research.

THE BROWN RAT

Night has fallen and all is calm in the farmhouse. The hens are sleepy. Perched in their hen house, they are silent, their heads beneath their wings. But beneath the floor of the hen house, a commotion starts up. As the world sleeps, the brown rats that built their nest here about five months ago wake up. Three lively young rats disrupt the grooming of the entire group. They jostle each other, nibble at one another, roll on top of each other, and begin a rowdy chase. Their mother calms them down by starting to groom them. Soon they all calm down. She keeps a careful eye on her last born, resting in a nest made of hay. Today the three young rats are going to leave the shelter where they have lived until now. They will explore the surroundings and learn how to find their own food. An older rat will be their guide. He is the oldest and most experienced member of the family. He is also an expert at detecting and avoiding the traps and poisoned bait left by the farmer. They all leave the shelter together.

The younger rats copy the older rat's movements exactly. They edge themselves into the crack that opens into the hen house. The last in line is completely distracted by everything it discovers. It stops in front of a hen that is sleeping on the lowest level of the perch. The young rat sniffs at the claws of the hen. Is this edible? Without hesitating, it begins to nibble at the claws to see what they taste like. Woken with a shock, the hen jumps away, screeching in fright. The noise wakes the rest of the hens and starts a concert of panicky screams.

Frightened, the young rat rapidly rejoins the other members of the group, which are rushing through the window into the basement of the farmhouse. The noises in the hen house stop. The farmer, who had rushed outside with rifle in hand, returns to bed, confused. As the noise quietens down, the rats head off in the direction of the pantry. There, the food is kept on shelves. But the farmer's wife has locked everything away in metal boxes. The young rats gnaw hopefully at the end of a tin to calm their hunger.

Then the older rat discovers a bottle of olive oil. Very quickly it takes off the cap, which had not been put back on correctly, and jumps on to a shelf above it. It dips its tail into the bottle just below it, takes it out and then lets the delicious liquid drip in the throats of the hungry young. What a feast!

LOCATION	DESCRIPTION	ENVIRONMENT	HABITS AND BEHAVIOUR	FOOD

LOCATION

- Originally from the Far East, the brown rat has spread throughout Europe since the 18th century. Today it is found all over the world, especially in **temperate** areas.

DESCRIPTION

- The head and body of the rat is 22-28 cm long.
- The length of its tail varies, but is often the same as the body.
- It weighs 250-600 g.
- Its fur is brownish-grey. The fur on its stomach is a whitish-grey colour. Rats' fur colour varies so that some brown rats look almost black.
- The tail has hardly any hair on it and looks naked.
- The brown rat is different from the black rat not just in fur colour, but also because it has shorter ears and a less pointed muzzle. The brown rat is also known as the wharf rat, the grey rat, the sewer rat and the migrating rat.

ENVIRONMENT

- The brown rat is found in the city (where they are numerous) and in the country. A few colonies are found in the countryside, where they live far from humans. But most brown rats live close to humans (in basements, slaughter-houses, markets, stables, hen houses, etc). They especially like damp environments, such as sewers. They dig holes beneath the floors or in the walls of houses.

HABITS AND BEHAVIOUR

- The brown rat lives in very **hierarchical** family groups. One group can include up to 200 individuals. Like mice, the members of the group recognise each other by smell.
- The importance of each rat is shown by their behaviour, which is either aggressive or submissive. Most rats do not have an aggressive temperament, and fighting between them is rare. The young in the colony are taught by the adults.
- Brown rats are especially active from dusk to dawn.
- When it feels threatened, a rat faces its enemy and defends its life. Its bites are vicious. It will attack cats and dogs that threaten it. Some of these animals are afraid of rats and will back off if faced with one.

FOOD

- The rat belongs to the rodent family. Like all rodents, as its front teeth wear down, they grow back again. This carries on throughout the animal's whole life.

- The rat is omnivorous. It eats seeds, foodstuffs, scraps, carcasses, fabrics, leather, paper, and so on. It may also attack small livestock. It can kill a chick or even a chicken or a pigeon. It especially likes eggs, and eats them swiftly without losing a drop. It usually does not store food and goes out each day in search of it.

REPRODUCTION

● The rat reproduces all year round, especially in spring and summer.
● The gestation period is three weeks long. The young are born naked and blind. They open their eyes after 5-6 days and are weaned at 3 weeks.
● The rate of reproduction is very high:
- a female can have up to 5 litters a year,
- a litter can be between 5-15 young,
- the females can breed at 11 weeks.
This explains why there can be more rats in a city than people. Their numbers only grow in relation to the available natural resources, such as food and shelter. This can limit the expansion of the rat population. But where conditions are perfect, the brown rat can reproduce very quickly.

ENEMIES

● The eagle owl and the stone marten are the rat's main predators in Europe.

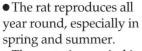

Vole

THE BROWN RAT AND PEOPLE

● The brown rat is a true pest for humans. It eats their food and makes what it does not eat unfit for consumption. It causes enormous damage by gnawing away at everything it finds in its path and mining through the foundations and walls of houses. It can also cause disasters, for example by attacking piping which starts flooding. Nearly half the fires started by short circuits are caused by the rat's taste for plastic wire coating. Babies and invalids have sometimes been injured by its bite.

● Rats have helped to spread diseases that have caused the death of millions of people. The bubonic plague is the best known. It can also carry typhus and rabies. The fight against the brown rat is not easy as it has learnt to avoid traps and poison.

Grey mouse

DANGERS

● These animals are under no threat whatsoever.

Brown rat

THE AFRICAN LOCUST

There is an atmosphere of celebration in the village. The date for a holiday has been set, which allows the children to help their families with the harvest that begins tomorrow. Their crops have finally grown in abundance in this region of Chad, which had suffered terribly from drought in the last few years. The surrounding fields are covered with corn and millet. Everyone is going to be able to eat as much as they want.

The playing children do not notice the sky darkening, like a cloud coming between the sun and the ground. A group of women, who were doing their laundry in the stream, suddenly appeared in the village. 'The locusts, the locusts are coming,' they shout.

Surprised, Boubé and his friend stand petrified. The elders of the village have told them a lot about the invasions of these devastating locusts. But so far, they had only been stories. 'Quick! Go! Help your parents. Quick!' shouts the leader of the village. Boubé does not need to hear it twice.

There are hundreds of insects around him, that he keeps swatting away from his body and crushing. The humming from the locusts' wings makes a dreadful racket. At last Boubé reaches his parents' fields. They are whirling cloths around in their hands like windmills. Weighed down by the water in which they had been soaked beforehand, the cloths act as clubs against the thieving locusts. In less than a minute, Boubé batters more than a hundred locusts that he crushes with a furious stamp of his foot. But the more he destroys, the more there are of them. There are millions landing on the crops, which they immediately devour. Boubé is completely surrounded by the horrible locusts. The cloud of insects finally goes away and the boy slumps down in the unnatural quiet. Everything in the area is devastated. Boubé searches for his garden, the small bit of land which his father had given him, and where he had planted the vegetables he was so proud of. There is nothing left. Heavy tears fall from his cheeks.

LOCATION	DESCRIPTION	ENVIRONMENT	HABITS AND BEHAVIOUR

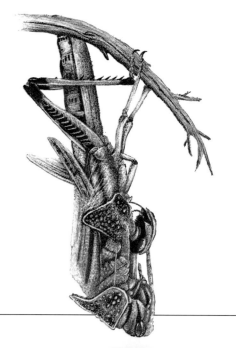

LOCATION

- The locust lives in north Africa and south-west Asia. It breeds in only one part of these areas: in Africa, Sudan, Chad, Nigeria, Mali, Mauritania; and in Asia, north of India, south of Yemen, and Saudi Arabia.

DESCRIPTION

- The locust is 6-8 cm long. The female is bigger than the male.
- It weighs 2-4 g.
- A young locust is pink and spotted with black. A mature locust is yellow spotted with black.
- It head has two short antennae and two large **compound eyes**.
- It has 6 legs. The two back ones are much larger than the others and allow the insect to jump. The wings are protected by covers. The larvae look like the adult insect, but are much smaller and have stumps instead of wings.

ENVIRONMENT

- The African locust lives in dry regions. But rain is important to them because they need **humidity to grow.** The larvae also need rich vegetation in water to develop.
- These conditions are only around at certain times of the year, in limited areas, for short periods of time. To find these places at the right time, the locusts have to migrate a long way.

HABITS AND BEHAVIOUR

- Locusts spend some of their lives living alone. During this time they pass unnoticed and they do not sing.
- When it begins to rain (which may not happen for long periods where the locust lives), the vegetation becomes abundant. During this time the locust changes its behaviour. It breeds very rapidly (about three generations can be born in three months).

- Locusts gather into huge groups. The larvae swarm around on the ground (they can't fly yet), while the adults can form groups of more than several thousand. When they fly they form clouds that can darken the sky. They can travel more than 1,000 km in this swarm.

DIET

● The locust is a herbivore (although grasshoppers are omnivorous). It has a huge appetite. As a larva, it eats the equivalent of its own weight each day. As an adult, it only eats half of it. It prefers the leaves of trees and small shrubs, as well as plants. It also eats the fruit, buds, and sometimes even the stems of plants.

REPRODUCTION

● The migratory locust can mate all year long. To attract a female, the male vibrates its wings. These vibrations do not produce any noise, but release a smell, that attracts the female. She then digs a deep hole in the ground, with her **abdomen**. She lays about a hundred eggs there.
● The larvae are born after about 10 days. To become an adult insect, a larva changes 5 times, moulting its skin each time to grow larger. Less than 20 days later it can breed.

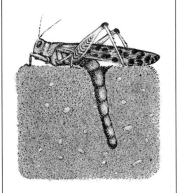

THE AFRICAN LOCUST AND PEOPLE

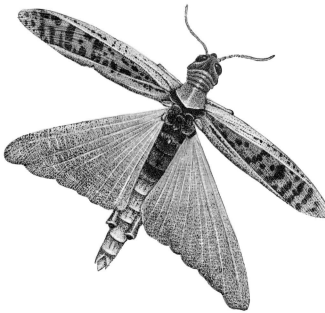

● In the Bible and the Koran, invasions of locusts are described as a divine curse. Locust swarms can devastate whole regions and cause famines which can be catastrophic. The damage they cause is dramatic, as it usually happens in regions that have suffered years of drought. The rain, when it comes, allows crops to grow again, but it also triggers off new swarms of locusts.

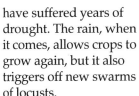

THE FIGHT AGAINST LOCUSTS

● The spraying of insecticides by plane on to the swarms kills a large number of insects. But insecticides also affect the birds, the livestock and the people that live in the treated areas.
● Prevention is the only way to fight against the invasions of locusts. The breeding areas need to be located and constantly watched. This is too expensive for the countries concerned and international organisations have become involved. Unfortunately, political problems such as wars in these countries have disrupted this preventative work.

THE STARLING

Two starlings walk around the field, dodging between the cows. After a few steps, they stop for a moment and with a careful glance, pull out the larvae of cranefly from their hiding places. When their beaks overflow with wriggling larvae, they fly rapidly to their nests in the neighbouring orchard. They place their findings in the wide open beaks of their six young and depart again to continue hunting.

The young starlings eventually leave the nest in the hollow apple tree and come out into the wider world. Curious and greedy for food, they peck away at everything they discover. The boldest already walk alongside their parents to be fed first on the rounds. In a few hours, they are able to fly. They are soon perched on the tree branches in the orchard, carefully inspecting everything. The father stabs into a well-ripened cherry and is soon copied by the nearest of its young. Another family of starlings joins them. Soon they are all enjoying the cherries. Instead of eating a few fruits, they peck a little from all the appetising-looking ones.

The damage to the orchard is serious. The farmer has been trying to move the birds away from the trees for several years. But his plans only last a short while. Not one of the starlings reacts to the explosions of the bird scarers he has placed in the orchard. Only his neighbours complain about the noise. One of the young starlings, curious about the scarer, approaches it.

All at once, there is panic in the group. Like a flash of lightning, a sparrow hawk has suddenly appeared in the sky and has swooped down on one of the young. This took only a few seconds. With the young starling tightly held in its claws, the bird of prey takes off, heading back to its territory. The starlings wheel around in the sky in a tight band. The danger of a new attack from the sparrow hawk makes them decide to choose another feasting ground and they soon take off.

LOCATION	DESCRIPTION	ENVIRONMENT	BEHAVIOUR

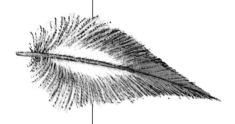

LOCATION

● The starling lives in most parts of Europe. It does not nest in the Iberian peninsula, Greece, on Mediterranean islands (where it has been replaced by the spotless starling) and some regions of Iceland, but it does spend the winter in these areas.

DESCRIPTION

● The starling measures 21 cm long.
● It weighs 80 g.
● It has black feathers with flecks of brown, purple, green and blue. In the winter it is spotted with beige and white. The chicks are dull brown.

● It has a short, stocky tail. Its beak is longer and more pointed than a blackbird's beak, and it has short legs. On the ground it trots quickly while shaking its head constantly. There is very little difference between the two sexes.

ENVIRONMENT

● Originally the starling was a forest bird.
● Today it can be seen everywhere, in cities, towns, woods and rocky regions. There are large numbers of starlings in **cultivated** areas.

BEHAVIOUR

● Starlings are very sociable. After the breeding season, flocks form of up to a million birds. When they fly, they form a kind of cloud. In the evening groups come together to spend the night in the same place.
● Its song is very varied. It is a combination of whistles, clucks, clinks, and a multitude of other noises. It can imitate the songs and cries of other species.

DIET

● Insects are the starling's basic diet. It eats a lot of the harmful larvae of the cranefly that it digs up in fields and lawns.
● It also has a taste for fruit. It is keen on cherries, apples, pears, grapes and elderberries.
● It is omnivorous and will eat all sorts of domestic scraps.

REPRODUCTION

● The starling searches for hollows in trees to nest. It reuses old nests chiselled out by woodpeckers. The gradual disappearance of old trees has not affected it as much as other hole-nesting species of birds. To raise its young, any hollow, natural or artificial, will do. It sets up its nest in the holes of walls, beneath the tiles of houses, in pits, or in a nesting box.
● The nest is made from leaves, straw and hay.
● The eggs are bright blue-green in colour and they lay about 5-8 in a clutch.
● The eggs are incubated for 22-25 days.
● The young leave the nest after 22-25 days. They stay in the same area for a few days, while their parents teach them how to look after and feed themselves.

THE STARLING AND PEOPLE

● The starling was once a pet bird. Today, it is not bred in captivity. Its spring song is attractive. On the other hand, its cries and the constant squawking of its young, begging for food, are annoying during breeding.
● When a flock of starlings swoops down on an orchard or a vineyard, it can completely wipe out a harvest in a few hours.
● The flight of flocks of starlings is very spectacular. But they can be dangerous at airports. If a bird is sucked into a jet engine, it can cause an air crash.
● Their nesting areas can be very noisy and smelly if there are a lot of birds in one place.
● For these reasons, people have often tried to kill starlings, shooting and trapping them. Some people even use poison and others have brought in the army to dynamite the birds' roosting areas. Nowadays these techniques are forbidden.

THEIR ROLE AND MEASURES FOR PROTECTION

Scientific studies have shown that starlings help people because they eat insects. Studies of swallows and other insect-eating birds show the same thing. Some of these birds have been legally protected for a long time. So why not starlings? Bird scarers can keep them away from farms. In some airports, birds of prey have been introduced to chase the starlings away. This keeps the starlings away from aeroplanes.

THE HERRING GULL

The gull looks like a dark shadow in the sky. As it glides in silence, it watches the colony of terns that are waiting excitedly for the first of their chicks to hatch. The gull's young hatched a little over a week ago and they are crying out for food.

The gull descends in circles from the sky and comes to rest on a rock. From its perch it examines the surroundings. Its keen, trained eye discovers a new chick on the edge of the terns' territory, even though this chick is motionless and its soft feathers camouflage it perfectly in its surroundings.

With a flap of its wings, the gull moves off its perch and flies towards its prey. It does not get very far. A hoard of terns takes off, screeching. They know the predator and have no intention of letting it kill. The terns outnumber the gull so they win. Without even seeing its attackers, the thief receives a volley of blows on the head. The pointed beak of the tern is a dangerous weapon, but the gull is larger and stronger. It tries to dodge its attackers and still makes for the chick.

The diving attacks of the terns become more frequent, and more precise. Harassed from all sides, the gull no longer feels safe and so it retreats. The victorious terns pursue it for a short while, and then quickly return to their nests.

Frustrated, the gull stops for an instant to preen its feathers. When it has finished, it flies off in a new direction. It lands on the grassy top of a cliff. The ground around it is full of burrows. It is the nesting site of puffins. One of the puffin parents returns from fishing. Small fish poke out of each side of its multicoloured beak. The puffin lands a safe distance from the gull and watches it uneasily. To reach its burrow and its young, the puffin must pass the gull. With small, careful steps, the puffin approaches the bigger bird. Then the gull attacks the puffin.

Frightened, the puffin tries to fly off. It has only gone two metres when it is caught by the gull. Seized by the feathers and the tail, and unbalanced, the puffin pirouettes in the air, opens its beak, and lets the fish it had caught for its young fall to the ground.

Immediately the gull abandons the puffin and flies to the ground to grab the fish. It gathers up its stolen booty and flies off to feed its hungry chicks.

LOCATION	DESCRIPTION	ENVIRONMENT	HABITS AND BEHAVIOUR

- The herring gull is found throughout Europe, in Asia and in North Africa.

- The gull is 55-60 cm long.
- Its wingspan is 1.4-1.6 m.
- The feathers on the gull's wings and back are grey, the tip of its wings are black and the rest of the body is white.
- Its beak is yellow and has a little red spot on its lower part.
- Its feet are webbed and yellow.
- The young birds have dark brown feathers spotted with light brown. It has adult plumage when it is four years old.

- At one time gulls were only found along coastlines and estuaries.
- Today they can be seen in lakes, rivers and even far inland.

- The herring gull can be seen alone or in groups. Gulls often fly in flocks.
- They follow fishing boats collecting scraps or catching small fish that escape from nets.
- They also follow ploughing tractors to seize worms and other invertebrates dug up by the plough.
- They find rubbish dumps a rich and easy source of food.
- A gull that finds a lot of food in one place attracts the attention of other gulls in the group which then gather round the food source.
- Gulls prey on mussel breeding areas. They carry the shellfish into the sky and then drop them so that their shells crack open.
- They raid colonies of terns and other seabirds, taking their eggs and chicks.
- Gulls attack puffins on their return from fishing trips, and force the puffins to drop their catch.
- They occasionally attack adult birds as well.

DIET

- Gulls are omnivorous. They eat everything they can find: fish, shellfish, domestic scraps, small mammals and birds.

REPRODUCTION

- Gulls usually nest in colonies.
- They prefer to settle on cliffs near other seabirds' colonies. They do not build nests but sometimes put together a few twigs.
- They lay 2-3 eggs on the ground.
- The two adults incubate the eggs alternately, but the female spends more time on the nest. The chicks are raised by both parents.
- The young can fly at about 6-7 weeks.

THE HERRING GULL AND PEOPLE

- Because the gull is adaptable, it has become very common. Mussel breeders and others want to limit its numbers. To encourage colonies of terns in areas where they were hunted by the herring gull, people have injected the gulls' eggs with a substance which makes them **sterile**. If these eggs were simply taken or destroyed, the birds would just lay a replacement egg.
- Flocks of several hundreds, or even thousands of gulls, have chosen ponds for resting places. The large quantity of excrement that they release causes damage to the water's natural balance and does as much harm to the plants as it does to the marine animal life in these ponds.

DANGERS AND MEASURES FOR CONSERVATION

- Despite the measures taken against it, the gull is not in danger of disappearing.

GLOSSARY

A

abdomen: the part of an animal's body that contains the digestive organs. In a mammal it is the belly and in an insect it is the last section of the body.

altitude: the height of land above the horizon. When you are on a mountain you are higher above the horizon than someone in the valley below. These different heights are known as altitudes.

aviary: a penned in area where birds are kept .

C

carnivore: an animal that eats meat.

carrier: an animal or person who can spread a disease but is not affected by it. So the fox will infect other animals with rabies, but will not suffer from it.

colony: a group of nesting animals, eg birds.

compound eye: an eye made up of lots of tiny eyes.

cultivated: land on which crops are grown.

D

dominant: an individual in a group which is more powerful than another. The leder of the pack is the most dominant of all.

E

embyro: an unborn, or unhatched offspring.

excrement: waste matter passed out by animals, for example, dung.

F

fertilise: when sperm meets the ovum (egg) to create new life.

G

gestation: the length of time it takes for offspring to develop inside the mother.

H

hierarchical: describing a group which has levels of importance within it.

humidity: the amount of moisture in air.

I

implanted: taken hold of or rooted into something.

incubation: the length of time it takes for offspring to develop in the egg.

invertebrates: animals that have no backbone.

L

larva: an immature form of an animal that will develop into an adult.

M

migration: a journey from one habitat to another at set times of the year, often to find food.

N

nocturnal: active at night.

O

on heat: a female animal which is ready to mate.

P

plumage: a bird's feathers.

predator: an animal that hunts and kills other animals for food.

prey: an animal that is hunted as food by another, called a predator.

S

sterile: to be unable to breed.

T

temperate: regions on the Earth that are neither very hot or very cold.

U

uterus: the place in the body of a female mammal where the young develop. It is also called a womb.

INDEX

Printed in Belgium